ANIMALS

Earthworms

by Kevin J. Holmes

Content Consultant:
Mark J. Wetzel
Associate Research Scientist
Illinois Natural History Survey, Center for Biodiversity

Bridgestone Books
an imprint of Capstone Press

Bridgestone Books are published by Capstone Press
818 North Willow Street, Mankato, Minnesota 56001
http://www.capstone-press.com

Library of Congress Cataloging-in-Publication Data
Holmes, Kevin J.
    Earthworms/by Kevin J. Holmes.
    p. cm.--(Animals)
    Includes bibliographical references (p. 23) and index.
    Summary: An introduction to earthworms' physical characteristics, habits, behavior, and
relationships to humans.
    ISBN 1-56065-744-8
    1. Earthworms--Juvenile literature. [1. Earthworms.] I. Title.
II. Series: Holmes, Kevin J. Animals.
QL391.A6H63   1998
592'.64--dc21

                                      97-31856
                                      CIP
                                      AC

Editorial Credits:
Editor, Martha E. Hillman; cover design, Timothy Halldin; photo research, Michelle L. Norstad

Photo Credits:
Dwight R. Kuhn, 10, 14, 18
Phillip Roullard, 4, 8, 16
Unicorn Stock Photos/Joel Dexter, 20
Visuals Unlimited, science, cover; Bill Beatty, 6; Barbara Gerlach, 12

Table of Contents

Segments

Clitellum

Tail

Head

Fast Facts

Kinds: There are more than 4,000 kinds of earthworms in the world.

Range: Earthworms live everywhere in the world except Antarctica.

Habitat: Most earthworms live underground in the soil. Some live under rocks, logs, or leaves.

Food: Earthworms eat rotting vegetables, plants, and grass. They eat dead animals and bugs.

Mating: Earthworms mate during spring and summer. They mate when the soil is moist and warm.

Young: Young earthworms hatch out of cocoons. They become adult earthworms in about 90 days.

Earthworms

Earthworms are invertebrates. An invertebrate is an animal that does not have a backbone. Their bodies are soft.

Earthworms are a kind of invertebrate called annelids. Most annelids are long invertebrates with segmented bodies. Segmented means made of many parts.

There are more than 4,000 kinds of earthworms in the world. More than 150 kinds live in North America.

Most earthworms are only about two to three inches (about five to eight centimeters) long. The longest earthworm is the Australian Gippsland. It grows as long as 10 feet (more than three meters). The longest earthworm in North America is the night crawler. Night crawlers grow as long as 12 inches (30 centimeters).

The largest earthworm in North America is the night crawler.

Appearance

Earthworms have long, thin bodies. They are pinkish-brown. They have no eyes, ears, or noses. They do not have legs.

Earthworm bodies have many segments. A segment is a part. The segments are shaped like rings. Adult earthworms have about 150 segments.

Earthworm bodies narrow to a point at each end. Their heads and their tails often look alike. Earthworm heads point forward when they crawl.

Earthworm skin is often wet. Their skin also has many chaetae. Chaetae are small hairs. Chaetae help earthworms move. Earthworms hold on to the ground with chaetae.

Every earthworm has a clitellum around its body. A clitellum is a band of swollen skin. The clitellum is a different color than other earthworm skin.

Earthworms have clitellums around their bodies.

Homes

Most earthworms live underground. They dig tunnels in soil. Sometimes they make burrows. A burrow is a hole in the ground where an animal lives. Other earthworms live under rocks, logs, or rotting leaves.

Earthworms breathe through their skin. They can breathe only in cool and wet conditions. This is why they usually come out at night. Earthworms can breathe easily in the cool, wet night air.

Earthworms avoid coming out when it is hot and sunny. Their skin hardens in hot, sunny weather. They cannot breathe when this happens.

Earthworms dig all year. They dig deep into the ground during summer and winter. In summer, they dig until they find wet soil. In winter, they dig until they find warm soil.

Earthworms dig tunnels in the ground.

Regeneration

Earthworms regenerate their tails or heads if they lose them. Regenerate means to grow again.

Earthworms can lose their heads or tails in several ways. Gardeners may cut them with shovels. Birds pull earthworms out of their tunnels. Earthworms hold on to the tunnel walls with their chaetae. They may hold on until their bodies break.

Regeneration does not always work. Earthworms die if they lose more than one-fourth of their bodies.

It is hard for earthworms to regenerate their heads. They cannot eat until their heads grow back. They become weak if they cannot eat. Enemies can catch them easily.

Birds pull earthworms out of their tunnels.

Eating and Enemies

Earthworms crawl on the surface of the soil to find food. They eat rotting vegetables, plants, leaves, and grass. Earthworms also eat dead animals and bugs.

Earthworms tunnel under the soil after they find food. They swallow soil with their food. Inside the earthworm, soil breaks the food into tiny pieces.

Earthworms have many enemies. Birds, ants, and lizards eat earthworms. Toads, frogs, snakes, and moles also eat earthworms. Sometimes moles store earthworms in their burrows to eat later.

Sometimes chaetae save earthworms from their enemies. The hairs help earthworms hold on to the sides of their tunnels. Enemies cannot easily pull earthworms out of the ground. Some enemies stop trying and leave earthworms alone.

Toads and frogs eat earthworms.

Mating

Earthworms mate during the spring and summer. Mate means to join together to produce young. The mating season begins when the soil is moist and warm.

Sometimes earthworms mate in their burrows. Other times they go to the surface. They mate with other earthworms there.

During mating, earthworms are next to each other. They face opposite directions. A sticky liquid comes out of their clitellums. The liquid forms a ring around their bodies. This ring helps their bodies stick together. Sticking together helps them mate. Mating takes about two or three hours.

Sometimes earthworms go to the surface to mate.

Young Earthworms

After mating, another sticky ring comes out of each earthworm's clitellum. This ring slides off the earthworm's body. It hardens into a small cocoon.

Eggs grow in the cocoon. Each cocoon holds between one and 20 eggs. Young earthworms hatch out of the cocoons after two to three weeks.

Young earthworms are thin and small. Otherwise, they look like adults. Most are one-half inch to one inch (1.3 to 2.5 centimeters) long.

Earthworms do not take care of their young. Young earthworms live on their own. They become adults in about 90 days. They keep growing until they are nine months old.

Many earthworms live only a few months. But some earthworms live for several years.

Earthworm eggs grow in cocoons.

Earthworms and People

Earthworms help people by keeping soil healthy. People need healthy soil to grow plants.

Earthworms dig burrows and tunnels in soil. This helps the soil take in water. Earthworms also keep soil loose. This makes it easier for plants to grow.

Earthworm waste is called castings. Earthworms leave their castings in the soil. Castings fertilize soil. Fertilize means to make soil rich. Plants grow well in fertilized soil.

Sometimes people hurt earthworms. They put poisons on the ground and on plants. The poisons kill harmful bugs. But the poisons also hurt earthworms. People can help earthworms by using fewer poisons on the soil.

Earthworms help people by keeping soil healthy.

Hands On: Light or Dark?

Earthworms live underground. You can find out if earthworms prefer light or darkness.

What You Need

Pan   Paper towels   Water

Earthworms   1 sheet of dark paper

What You Do

1. Ask an adult to help you find some earthworms. Look in gardens, under leaf piles, or under rocks.
2. Wet the paper towels. Put the damp paper towels on the bottom of the pan.
3. Cover half of the pan with dark paper. Leave the other half open to light.
4. Put an earthworm in the middle of the pan. Watch which way it goes.
5. Repeat the test with other earthworms.
6. Put the earthworms back outside in the soil.

Where do most of the earthworms go? Remember that earthworms live in darkness. Most of them should go to the dark side of the pan.

Words to Know

annelid (AN-uh-lid)—a long invertebrate with a segmented body

burrow (BUR-oh)—a hole in the ground where an animal lives

castings (KAST-ings)—earthworm waste

chaetae (KEE-tee)—small hairs on an earthworm's body

clitellum (cli-TEL-lum)—a swollen band around an earthworm; used in mating

fertilize (FUR-tuh-lize)—to make soil rich

invertebrate (in-VUR-tuh-brit)—an animal without a backbone

mate (MATE)—to join together to produce young

regenerate (re-JEN-uh-rate)—to grow again

segmented (SEG-men-tuhd)—made of many parts

Read More

Merrick, Patrick. *Earthworms*. Chanhassen, Minn.: Child's World, 1998.

Pascoe, Elaine. *Earthworms*. Woodbridge, Conn.: Blackbirch Press, 1997.

Useful Addresses

Canadian Society of Soil Science
General Delivery
Pinawa, Manitoba R0E 1L0
Canada

Worm Digest
P.O. Box 544
Eugene, Oregon 97440

Internet Sites

The Burrow
http://gnv.fdt.net/~windle
Worm Woman's Web Site
http://www.wormwoman.com
Worm World
http://www.nj.com/yucky/worm

Index